Reproducibles, Activities, And Ideas To Develop

Critical Thinking

For the Primary Grades

by Laurie Rozakis

SCHOLASTIC
PROFESSIONAL BOOKS

New York • Toronto • London • Auckland • Sydney

With love and thanks, I dedicate
this book to all the fine teachers
who have enriched my life:
Barbara Bengels, Chris LaRosa,
Ed Leigh, Jack McGrath,
Jim Pepperman, Jennifer Richmond,
Elizabeth Simmons, Lenore Strober,
and Tom Thibadeau.

Designed by Nancy Metcalf
Production by Intergraphics
Cover design by Vincent Ceci
Cover art by Beth Glick
Illustrations by Anna Cota Robles

ISBN 0-590-49161-X

Contents

Introduction

Critical thinking is neither innate nor naturally acquired; we are not born with the ability to think critically nor do we simply pick it up. In fact, only about half the adults in America today have the ability to reflect upon their thinking and explain how they solved a problem. The good news? Critical thinking *can* be taught. This book is designed to help you teach your students to reflect on their own thinking processes, and in so doing, become more successful, active learners.

In our daily lives we use many critical thinking skills simultaneously—and not in a prescribed order. For the purposes of this book, however, activities are arranged in a hierarchy, so that you and your students can more clearly understand and identify the specific critical thinking skills they are using.

To follow are some suggestions for using the lessons in this book to help you help children become better thinkers:

1. Read each activity aloud or have a student read it.
2. Ask the students questions to encourage and assess their understanding of the problem.
3. Solicit possible strategies for finding a solution.
4. Observe and question what children are doing.
5. Give helpful hints to those students who seem to be having difficulty.
6. Encourage children to relate the problem to others they have already solved.
7. Allow children ample time to think and respond.
8. Urge students to check their work and the reasoning behind it.
9. Discuss the solutions that individual students reach.
10. Encourage children to identify the different strategies they used to solve the problem.

Since critical thinking does not end when the project does, give students time to evaluate their thinking strategies. Explore with them how they might adjust their strategies the next time around.

Finally, try to model critical thinking for your students by welcoming your own preconceptions and accepting unusual and unexpected strategies and solutions. Your participation as an active learner will further reinforce the critical thinking skills you teach. Above all, encourage your students to think of themselves as thinkers.

Recognizing and Recalling

To begin to think critically, children must first learn to recognize and recall information. The activities in this section are designed to help kids learn how to tap their prior knowledge. You can present any combination of these activities as a complete lesson or, alternatively, you can use one or more as the introduction and/or conclusion to a critical thinking lesson.

In addition, many of the activities in this section can easily be integrated into other content areas. "I Like You" (page 10), "In or Out?" (page 11), and "Map a Person" (page 17) are literature-based; "Home Sweet Home" (page 13) and "Animals, Animals" (page 16) work well with social studies or science. Other activities, such as "On My Own" (page 15), help children build self-confidence and self-esteem.

Quick Change Game

To introduce children to the critical thinking skills of recognition and recalling, sit the entire class in a circle. Make sure everyone has a clear view of the center.

Explain to the class that this game will test their ability to remember what someone looks like and to recognize any changes in their appearance.

Next, ask two volunteers to stand in the center of the circle. Give them ten to twenty seconds to study each other closely. Then have them turn their backs on each other and change three things about their appearance. Changes can be subtle—removing a barrette from their hair or untying a sneaker—or more obvious—taking off a pair of glasses or removing a sneaker, for instance. Have the volunteers turn around to face each other. Give them ten to twenty seconds to find all the changes in each other's appearance. When their time is up, have volunteers state whether their partner's observations were correct. Continue the game using new pairs of volunteers until everyone in the class has had a chance in the circle.

As the game progresses, you can reduce the time, increase the number of changes, and suggest that children make their changes more subtle.

Mirror, Mirror

Here is another enjoyable and effective activity to help children develop recognition and recalling skills. Begin by exploring with the class what they see when they look in a mirror. You might want to bring in a hand or wall mirror to help children understand just how a mirror works. Then explain to the class that in this game they will be each others' "mirrors." They will have to look very carefully at someone so they can reflect exactly what they are seeing.

Arrange children in pairs. (Include yourself if one child needs a partner.) Have partners face each other. Select one child in each pair to be the "image," the other to act as the "mirror." Ask the "image" to make a happy face and have the "mirror" copy it. Then have the "image" make a sad face and have the "mirror" copy it. Next ask "images" to slowly move their face, arms, legs, and body so "mirrors" can copy them. Repeat the activity, reversing the roles of "image" and "mirror" so that all children have a chance to play both parts.

I Like You

With the class, share Arnold Lobel's *Frog and Toad Are Friends* (HarperCollins) or any other grade-appropriate book that talks about friends. Then ask kids to complete this sentence:

A friend is _____ .

List their ideas on the board and discuss the various ways friends show they care. Encourage them to recall specific ways friends have acted toward them. Children might suggest that friends help each other by sharing snacks and toys, and by talking about their feelings.

Then ask children to form a "friendship circle" by sitting in a circle and linking hands. Join the circle yourself. One at a time, have children turn to the person next to them and say something nice about them, such as "I like the way you share the crayons" or "I like the way you sing."

To complete the lesson, teach children the lyrics to this traditional friendship song and discuss its meaning: "Make new friends, but keep the old; one is silver and the other gold."

In or Out?

Here is a literature-based activity to help children develop their recognition and recalling skills. Select a story that children have read or that you have read to them. You might want to reread the story to the class before you begin to make sure that children are familiar with it.

Explain to students that you are going to list details on the board from the story. Some of the details will really come from the story; others will not. Ask children to identify which details come from the story. Here is a sample list from Syd Hoff's *Danny and the Dinosaur* (Harper and Row):

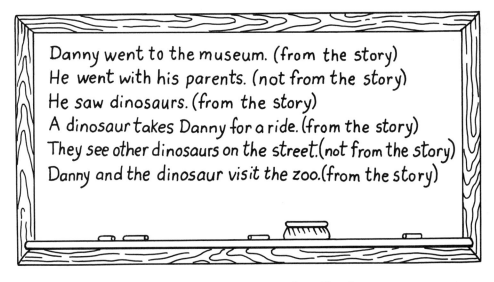

Danny went to the museum. (from the story)
He went with his parents. (not from the story)
He saw dinosaurs. (from the story)
A dinosaur takes Danny for a ride. (from the story)
They see other dinosaurs on the street. (not from the story)
Danny and the dinosaur visit the zoo. (from the story)

Then ask children to add two more details that come from the story. For example, for *Danny and the Dinosaur* they might add that Danny gives the children a ride on the dinosaur, Danny learns tricks, or Danny plays hide and seek.

Continue this activity by having children work in pairs or small groups to make up a list of details from another story the class has read, adding two or three details that they have "invented" themselves. Have each team present their lists to the class. Encourage other students to distinguish between details that come from the story and details that do not.

Alphabet Soup

Here's an activity that's both educational and delicious! Ask students to work individually or in pairs to form as many words as they can from pasta or breakfast cereal letters. For beginning readers, allow at least five minutes for each round; allow less time for more advanced readers.

Before class, sort through the letters to pick out those suitable for forming simple words. For beginning readers, for example, select letters such as *C, A, T, D, O,* and *G.* For more advanced readers, select letters needed to form more complex words. For an extra challenge, you may wish to have children pick out a handful of letters at random. Regardless of grade level, make sure everyone has enough letters to form words they know.

Then tell children that they will have a certain amount of time in which to form as many words as they can with their letters. Explain that they do not have to use all the letters for each word, and that words can have as few as one letter. No fair biting off parts of an *E* to make an *F*! Ask children to write down each word as they form it, since the letters may move around. When time is up, have volunteers list their letters and the words they formed on the board. Then invite the rest of the class to look at the words on the board and contribute any additional ones they can think of.

At the end of the activity, children can eat the cereal letters and glue their pasta words onto a sheet of paper.

Home Sweet Home

Draw a picture of an animal that would live in each home. Next to the animal, draw what it likes to eat.

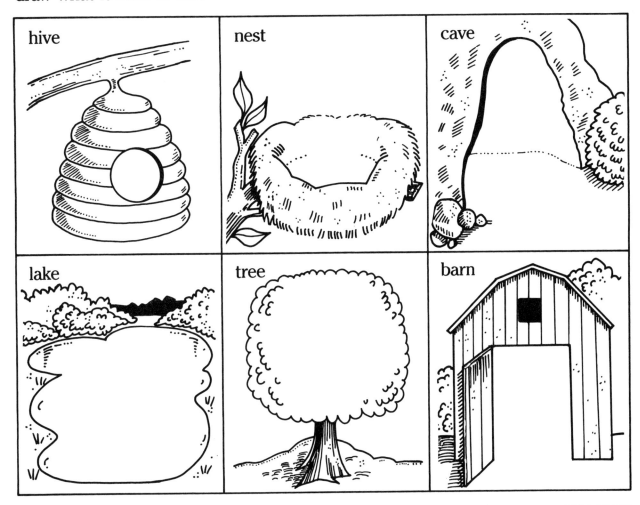

Now draw *your* home!
Draw yourself inside.

Happy, Sad, and Mad

What things make you happy? What things make you sad? What things make you mad?

On the lines below, write five things that make you happy, five things that make you sad, and five things that make you mad.

Things that Make Me Happy:	**Things that Make Me Sad:**	**Things that Make Me Mad:**
1. _____	1. _____	1. _____
2. _____	2. _____	2. _____
3. _____	3. _____	3. _____
4. _____	4. _____	4. _____
5. _____	5. _____	5. _____

Write a Story: Select one thing you wrote from any of the columns. Then write a short story telling more about why this thing makes you happy, sad, or mad.

Name _____

On My Own

Think of the things that you have learned to do by yourself. What a long list! Now fill in the blank to complete each sentence.

I can do many things on my own.

On my own, I can _____

On my own, I can _____

On my own, I can _____

On my own, I can _____

On my own, I can _____

On my own, I can _____

Write Your Thoughts: Choose one thing you wrote about that is still difficult for you to do by yourself. Write a few sentences explaining why.

15

Name _____

Animals, Animals

In the space below, draw as many animals as you can that are bigger than you.	In the space below, draw as many animals as you can that are green.
In the space below, draw as many animals as you can that live in the zoo.	In the space below, draw as many animals as you can that live in a house.
In the space below, draw as many animals as you can that are smaller than you.	In the space below, draw as many animals as you can that have fur.

Map a Person

Choose a character from a story you read. Think about that person. What was that person like? Which parts of the story told you about the person? To help you describe the person, complete the map below.

Story _____

What I learned about the person:	What I learned about the person:
_____ _____	_____ _____

Part of story:	Part of story:
_____ _____	_____ _____

Person's name:

_____

Part of story:	Part of story:
_____ _____	_____ _____

What I learned about the person:	What I learned about the person:
_____ _____	_____ _____

Snapdragon!

We can put words together to make other words. These new words are called *compound words.* See how many compound words you can make. Draw lines to connect these words.

day	self
foot	time
my	side
out	light
some	ball

no	tan
every	ball
how	one
sun	body
hand	ever

ice	one
in	burn
some	cube
no	body
sun	side

rain	pal
pine	light
pen	body
sun	cone
every	bow

Make More Words: Work with two classmates. Using the words on this page, try to think of other compound words that you haven't already put together.

Bunch Up

People like to eat different kinds of fruit. What about you? Which fruits do you like? Which fruits don't you like?

On the bottom of the page are pictures of different fruits. Cut out the pictures. Then place them in the correct bowls.

Fruits I Like to Eat   **Fruits I Do Not Like to Eat**

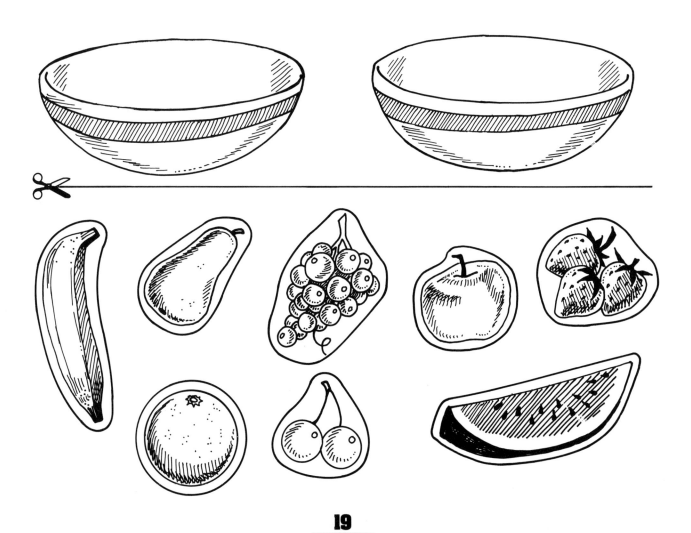

A Is for...

So many things grow! Write something that grows for each letter. It might be a fruit, a vegetable, a tree, a plant, a flower, or an animal. The first one is done for you.

A is for _apples_____

L is for _____

B is for _____

M is for _____

C is for _____

N is for _____

D is for _____

O is for _____

E is for _____

P or Q is for _____

F is for _____

R is for _____

G is for _____

S is for _____

H is for _____

T is for _____

I is for _____

U or V is for _____

J is for _____

W is for _____

K is for _____

X, Y, or Z is for _____

Make a new A, B, C list for things that move. For each letter, write one thing that moves.

Distinguishing and Visualizing

When children become skilled at distinguishing between important and unimportant data and visualizing problem-solving strategies, they tend to develop more logical and effective thinking patterns.

You might want to give children a little extra time to work through each of the activities in this section. Research shows that children answer questions more thoughtfully and completely when they are given ample time to work. Children might especially benefit from extra time with "Break-Aparts," (page 25), "Near Match" (page 28), "Hands On!" (page 32), and "Look Up! Look Down!" (page 33).

Name _____

Dish It Out!

Which ice-cream treats are which? Draw a line from the picture to the words that tell about it. Then color the ice cream you like the best!

Who put a straw in my glass?

There's no whipped cream in my dish!

I have an extra scoop of ice cream!

Marie ate my cherry!

Charles put his spoon in already!

I have 3 scoops of ice cream, a cherry, and whipped cream!

Draw your own super ice-cream treat in the dish below. Color your picture, too.

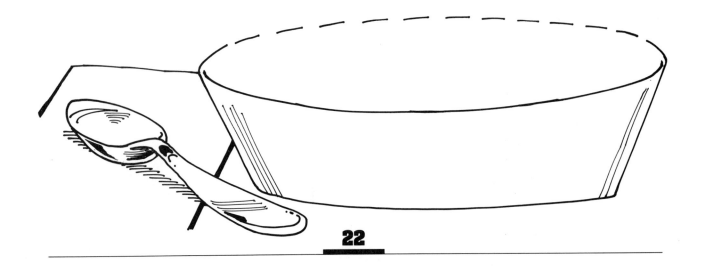

Pumpkin Face

Draw a line from the pumpkin to the words that tell about it. Then color the pumpkin you like the best.

My nose is square.

My nose is round.

I have eyebrows.

I don't have a nose.

I don't have a mouth.

I am sad.

Jack carved a pumpkin. The eyes are square. Jack made triangles for eyebrows. It did not have a nose. The pumpkin's mouth was round. It had three teeth, one on top and two on the bottom. Draw Jack's pumpkin on this table.

Mixed-Up Zoo

These zoo animals' names are all mixed up. Put the letters in the right order.
Then write the name of each animal under its picture.

gerit	niol	ynokem
easkn	bezar	reab

_____   _____

_____   _____

_____   _____

Break-Aparts

All the words in these sentences are pushed together. Break them apart and read the sentences. Then write the words on the lines.

1. Ilikedogs. _____

2. Wehaveadog. _____

3. Heisbig. _____

4. Doyoulikedogs? _____

5. Thisisabusyday. _____

6. Eatallyourlunch. _____

7. Savemeaseat. _____

8. Whereisyourhouse? _____

9. Doyouliketoswim? _____

10. Weswiminalake. _____

11. Thelakeiscold. _____

12. Iswimveryfast. _____

13. InwinterIskate. _____

14. Thelakeisfrozen. _____

 Write some "break-aparts" to stump your classmates.

Color My World

Circle all the names of colors that are hidden in this puzzle. The colors may be written up, down, or across.

Here are the colors in the puzzle:

violet
tan
lime
black
blue
green
orange
purple
white
yellow
pink
red
brown
silver

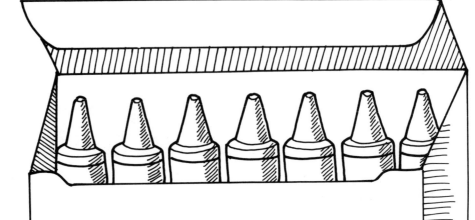

```
b r o w n b o r a n g e s
l i m e t l e g y v r d i
u w h d a a d o e i e w l
e p u i n c w l l o e h v
y u p i n k h d l l n i e
w h i t e x i o o e p t r
p u r p l e t s w t r e d
```

What's Going On Here?

What is wrong with the pond? Circle 12 things that are wrong.

Draw a picture of a park. Draw some things that really belong in a park and some things that don't. Ask a friend to tell which things belong and which ones don't.

Near Match

These two chairs match.
They are the same in every way.

These two chairs *almost* match.
They are both chairs, but they are
not the same.

In this picture there are ten pairs of things that *almost* match. Circle each pair.
Draw a line to connect each set. The first one has been done for you.

Small, Smaller, Smallest

Read the four words in each line. Circle the word that describes the smallest thing.

1. pin	peanut	bed	bird
2. apple	orange	truck	grape
3. fork	spoon	snowflake	bridge
4. car	mop	pie	ice cube
5. house	door	cherry	fly
6. river	ocean	cup	coat
7. swan	frog	camel	elephant
8. turtle	deer	duck	bee
9. rose	tree	kite	sun
10. rat	bean	hat	airplane

Now put a box around the largest thing in each line.

In the three boxes draw something that is small, something that is smaller, and something that is the smallest of all.

small	smaller	smallest

It's Handy!

Read each word. Decide if the word describes something smaller or bigger than your hand. If the word describes something smaller, circle the word *smaller*. If the word describes something bigger, circle the word *bigger*.

1. desk	smaller	bigger		**6.** nose	smaller	bigger
2. pen	smaller	bigger		**7.** tree	smaller	bigger
3. jelly bean	smaller	bigger		**8.** quarter	smaller	bigger
4. monkey	smaller	bigger		**9.** mother	smaller	bigger
5. paper clip	smaller	bigger		**10.** bean	smaller	bigger

Trace your hand in the space below. Then fill it in with drawings of things that are smaller than your hand.

Name _____

Super Shapes

Look at the shapes on this page. Then think of some things that are these shapes. Write those things on the lines below the matching shape.

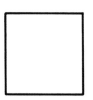

1. _____

2. _____

3. _____

4. _____

5. _____

1. _____

2. _____

3. _____

4. _____

5. _____

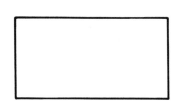

1. _____

2. _____

3. _____

4. _____

5. _____

1. _____

2. _____

3. _____

4. _____

5. _____

Hands On!

Your hands are pretty handy! They can do a lot of things. Look what they can do:

You know what hands can do. What can hands *be*? In the space below, trace your right hand or your left hand.

Now make your hand shape into something else. You can make an animal, a flower, or a flag. You can make a boat, a person, or a tree. You can make anything you want!

Look Up! Look Down!

Pretend you are a giant.
What things could you do? Write your answer here:

_____

_____

_____

_____

_____

Pretend you are as small as an ant. What things could you do?
Write your answer here:

_____

_____

_____

_____

_____

Write a Story: Write a story about a person who is as big as a giant or as small as an ant. Give a name to your person.

Name _____

Wacky Words

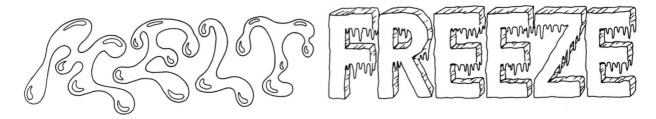

Look at the word *melt*. It looks like it's melting! And look at *freeze*. It looks like it's freezing! Pick five words from the list below. Write the words in the box. Make them look like what they tell about.

fast	boil	happy	sad	angry
hot	cold	funny	strange	mean
windy	slice	sharp	crack	fry

Following Directions and Classifying

After children feel comfortable distinguishing and visualizing different aspects of a problem, it is time for them to work on following directions and classifying information. The ability to follow directions helps children work through a process one step at a time. Knowing how to classify information helps them to bring order to a problem by organizing its pieces into groups based on similarities.

Each of the activities in this section guides children through the processes of following directions and classifying. Consider presenting one or more of the activities at the beginning of the day on a daily basis, to alert students to the importance of following directions with regard to *all* their work. Children can work on the activities either individually, in pairs, or in small groups.

As children complete the activities, encourage them to think aloud. This will help you to observe the thought processes children are using. Suggest that children think aloud as they work through "Clean up Time" (page 42), "Where Can You Find It?" (page 43), and "Cross It Out" (page 44) in particular.

Directing Directions

Although following directions is difficult for many students, it is one of the cornerstones of successful critical thinking. Before you present any of the activities in this section, consider beginning with the following activity.

Give students several simple oral directions, such as:
○ Stand up and raise your arms over your head.
○ Blink your eyes twice.
○ Touch your right ear with your left hand.

Increase the directions in length and complexity. Start by allowing students to complete one direction before you give the next. Then give several directions at once and ask students to carry them out.

Finally, write simple multi-step directions on index cards or slips of paper. Hand one to each student and give them a few moments to read what you have written. Then have students take turns carrying out the directions they have received. After each student has performed the required tasks, have the rest of the students write down what they believe the directions were. For instance:

○ Stand up. Hop three steps. Touch your nose. Walk backwards to your seat. Do not sit down.
○ Stand up. Jump twice. Wave to me. Reach for the ceiling. Go back to your seat. Sit down.

Note that children who have difficulty remembering steps or have trouble with gross motor coordination may need to have appropriate modifications made.

As a variation, have students write simple directions for their classmates to follow. After each student has performed the tasks, ask others to write what they believe the directions were.

Listen and Recognize

To help children following directions and classify, try this listening activity. The object of this exercise is to encourage children to follow directions and classify words according to their vowel sounds.

Tell children that you are going to say some pairs of words. If both words in the pair have the vowel sound /ē/, as in *bee* and *tree,* they should hold their thumbs up. If both words in the pair do not have the vowel sound /ē/, they should put their thumbs down. (You may want to write *bee* and *tree* on the chalkboard to remind children of the sound they are listening for.) Here are some word pairs you can use:

○ *feel/mean* (thumbs up)   ○ warms/see (thumbs down)
○ *read/keep* (thumbs up)   ○ rain/stain (thumbs down)
○ jump/cook (thumbs down)   ○ *jeep/leap* (thumbs up)
○ *she/steam* (thumbs up)   ○ tot/pop (thumbs down)
○ me/men (thumbs down)   ○ *peace/knee* (thumbs up)
○ *street/neat* (thumbs up)   ○ grew/many (thumbs down)

Continue the activity with other sounds, such as /ō/. If both words in the pair have the vowel sound /ō/, as in *coat* and *goat,* children should hold their thumbs up. If both words in the pair do not have the sound /ō/, they should put their thumbs down. Here are some word pairs you can use:

○ *float/boat* (thumbs up)   ○ fog/log (thumbs down)
○ *moat/poke* (thumbs up)   ○ fat/sat (thumbs down)
○ bog/beg (thumbs down)   ○ *soak/row* (thumbs up)
○ *soap/cope* (thumbs up)   ○ bake/cake (thumbs down)
○ look/cool (thumbs down)   ○ *goat/rope* (thumbs up)
○ *choke/joke* (thumbs up)   ○ lake/mat (thumbs down)

Children might want to continue this activity by adding thumbs-up word pairs to each of the lists.

On the Beat

This activity encourages students to follow directions and classify words in a sentence by sharpening their listening skills.

Label each of five large cards with one of the following words: *Who? What? Where? When? Why?* Divide the class into five teams and give each team one of the cards to hold. Explain to students that you will read a sentence aloud and then you will give them a key word or phrase from the sentence. If the key word or phrase corresponds to the question *Who?*, the *Who* team members should raise their hands; if the key word or phrase corresponds to the question *What?*, the *What* team members should raise their hands, and so on. For example, if you read the sentence "Marianne went to visit her grandmother in Alaska" and you choose the key word *Alaska*, the *Where* team members should raise their hands.

You may want to use sentences from children's reading, classroom experience, or daily events. By choosing different key words, you can use each sentence more than once. Try to offer a variety of key words so that each group gets a chance to participate.

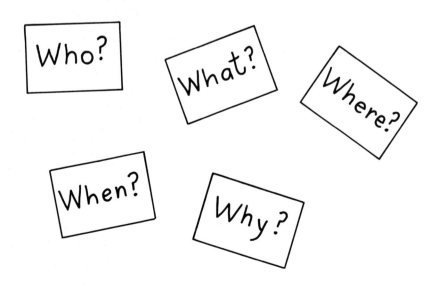

Like It or Not!

Read Lois Lowry's *Anastasia Krupnik* (Bantam Skylark) to your students and discuss how Anastasia created lists of things she loved and things she hated. Discuss with students how her lists changed over the course of the story. Next ask students to name things they like and things they dislike. Write their responses on the board. As the list grows, have children explain how their tastes have changed over the years. What things do they like now that they disliked in the past? What things do they dislike now that were favorites in the past?

Arrange the items on the board in categories, such as food, animals, activities, games, cartoon characters, and tv shows. Then have students create their own lists of likes and dislikes. When lists are complete, ask students to classify items as follows:

Category: food

Things I Like	Things I Do Not Like
1. corn	1. beets
2. apples	2. orange soda
3. chocolate	3. grape jelly
4. fried chicken	4. liver
5. peanut butter	5 pickles

Name _____

Read First!

Read *all* the directions on this page before you do anything. Read *all* the way to the end of the paper before you do anything.

1. Write your name on the top of this paper.

2. Write your name at the top of a blank sheet of paper.

3. Say an animal's name, like *cow* or *pig*.

4. Draw a picture of the animal you said.

5. Draw the animal's home.

6. Write the animal's name.

7. Stand up, turn around three times, and clap your hands two times.

8. Sit down and touch your left ear.

9. Stand up, touch your toes without bending your knees, and sit down.

10. Write the name of a person you like.

11. Draw a picture of that person and write the person's name.

12. Read three pages in any one of your books.

13. Put your head down on the desk and rest for a minute.

14. Draw a picture of your classroom.

15. Write the day, month, and year.

16. Write down something you want to do this weekend.

17. Stand up, reach for the sky, and sit down.

18. Stand up, hop on your left foot four times, and sit down.

19. Draw a picture of you when you are thinking.

20. Do only step 1 and step 20. Then put your head down on the desk.

 **Try This**

Write More: Write 10 directions like the ones above. Ask a classmate to read and follow them. See if they can follow directions.

Help This Picture!

This picture needs help! Read these clues. Then finish the picture.

1. Draw a boy on the bed.
2. Draw a table next to the bed.
3. Put a glass of milk on the table.
4. Draw a book on the table, too.
5. Put blue curtains on the window.
6. Draw the sun in the window.

7. Draw a cat on the floor. The cat is far away from the bed.
8. Give the cat a toy to play with. The toy is green.
9. Make the walls yellow.
10. Color the rug your favorite color.

Clean-Up Time

What a mess! Time to put the clothes away. You have two closets in your room. It's up to you to decide where the clothes go. Draw a picture of each piece of clothing in the closet where you think it belongs. Think of a name for each of your groups and write it on the line.

robe	coat	scarf	boots
slippers	pants	hat	pajamas
mittens	shoes	socks	shirt

Closet 1　　　　　　　　　　　**Closet 2**

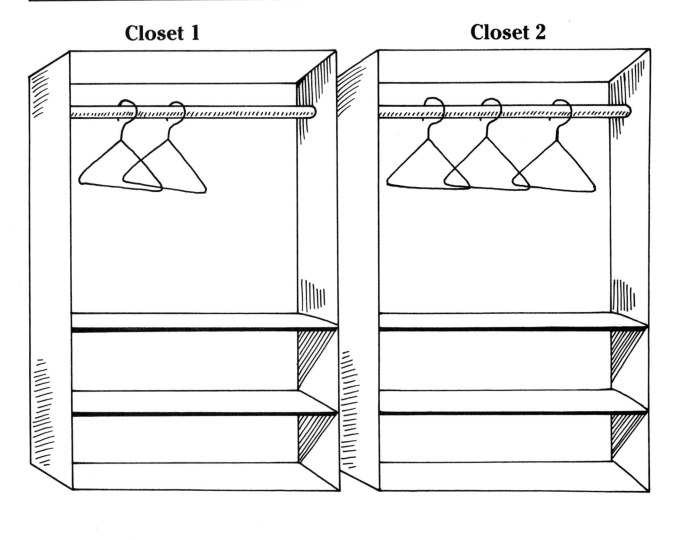

_____　　　_____
Name of group　　　　　　　　　Name of group

Where Can You Find It?

Draw a circle around the things you would find at the park. Draw a box around the things you would find at school. If you think something can be found in both places, draw a circle and a box around it.

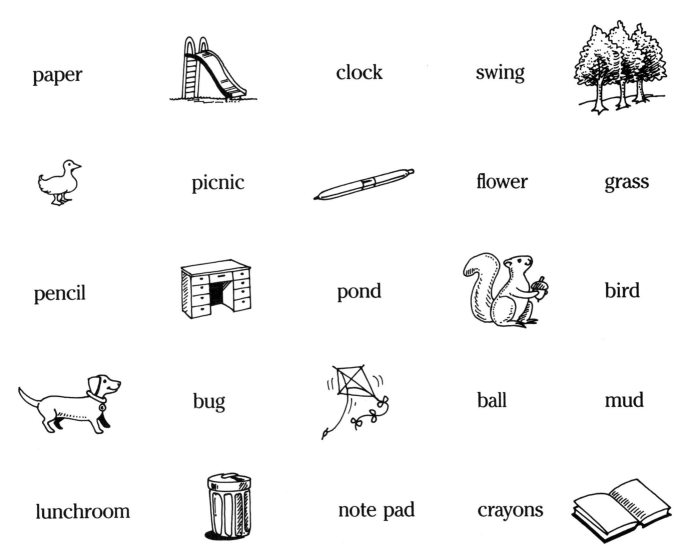

paper   clock   swing

picnic   flower   grass

pencil   pond   bird

bug   ball   mud

lunchroom   note pad   crayons

List some things you would find at the grocery store. List some things you would find at home. Scramble up the words in the two lists. Give them to a classmate to sort into the right groups.

Cross It Out!

On each line there is a word that does not fit. Cross out the word that does not belong to the group.

Example: **apple**   **pear**   **grape**   ~~**bean**~~

Apple, pear, and *grape* are all fruits. *Bean* does not belong to the group because it is not a fruit. After crossing out the word that does not belong to the group, write the name of the group on the line.

Name of Group

1. nurse	father	mother	brother	_____
2. socks	ice	hat	shoes	_____
3. red	blue	green	paint	_____
4. head	pen	foot	ear	_____
5. plant	tree	flower	cloud	_____
6. book	pen	pencil	crayon	_____
7. snow	rain	sleet	summer	_____
8. sled	horse	cow	pig	_____
9. peas	corn	potato	peach	_____
10. sleep	good	eat	run	_____
11. orange	open	over	green	_____
12. bee	fly	worm	beetle	_____
13. steam	ice	snow	frost	_____
14. ocean	lake	desert	river	_____
15. pancake	record	map	ball	_____

Great Groups

Each row has four things. Three things belong together. One thing does not. Cross out the thing that does not fit. Then look at the words at the bottom of the page. Find the one that will help you complete each sentence. Write it in the blank.

1. These three things are found _____

2. These three things are found _____

3. These three things are found _____

4. These three things are found _____

5. These three things are found _____

6. These three things are found _____

○ in a kitchen   ○ at the beach   ○ in a closet

○ in a toolbox   ○ in an office   ○ in your class

What Is What?

Read the words in each box. Look at the pictures in each box. Then follow the directions.

These are vehicles.

These are not vehicles.

Color the vehicles.

These are zorks.

These are not zorks.

Color the zorks.

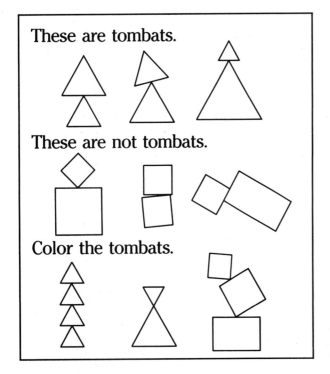

These are tombats.

These are not tombats.

Color the tombats.

These are lorks.

These are not lorks.

Color the lorks.

Sequencing and Predicting

One of the most important steps in the critical thinking process is the ability to sequence details and predict information based on prior knowledge. The activities in this section are designed to further develop these skills in children.

Studies have shown that children who work in pairs or small groups tend to come up with more thoughtful responses. Therefore, you should consider trying a collaborative approach to some of these activities, such as "Busy Day" (page 52), "Lunch Time" (page 53), and "Happily Ever After?" (page 56).

Goodnight!

Read *Goodnight, Moon* by Margaret Brown (HarperCollins) to your students. Then discuss with them the things they could say goodnight to before they go to sleep. Children might suggest their stuffed animals, toys, and books, for example. Write some of the words they volunteer on the board.

Next have children make their own "goodnight" books. Give each child two or three pieces of paper folded in half lengthwise and stapled together. Ask children to write *Goodnight* __(blank)__ on each page and to fill in the blank and illustrate the word they wrote. Children might enjoy sharing their books by reading to a partner, the class, or their parents.

Who's On First?

Here's another way to help children learn to sequence ideas. Begin by having children brainstorm a list of tasks they perform around the classroom, such as watering plants cleaning the chalkboards, or acting as line leader. Explain that each task entails several different steps, and briefly discuss some of the steps in each process.

Then divide the class into small groups. Assign each group a task from the list they brainstormed. Have each group break down the task into four steps and write down each step on a separate piece of paper. Then ask children to mix up the order of the papers. Invite each group to present their mixed-up process to the rest of the class. Ask the class to correctly sequence the steps and to make any suggestions for other ways to break down or sequence the task.

When each group has finished its presentation and all revisions have been completed, make a class chart of each task and process, correctly ordered. Display the chart in a prominent place in the classroom and use it to have children complete the tasks.

		CLASS TASKS		
S T E P S		WATERING PLANTS		CLEANING CHALKBOARDS
	1	Get pitcher from shelf.	1	Erase chalkboard with eraser.
	2	Fill pitcher with water.	2	Wash board with sponge.
	3	Water all plants except cactus!	3	Clean chalkboard ledge with rag.
	4	Pour out extra water and put pitcher away.	4	Clap chalk dust out of erasers.

Brush Your Teeth!

Below are six things you do when you brush your teeth. First draw a picture for each thing. Then cut out the pictures and put them in order. Last, staple the pictures together to make a little book.

Squeeze the toothpaste onto the brush.	Rinse your mouth with water.	Brush your teeth.
Get your toothbrush and the toothpaste.	Put the brush inside your mouth.	Put the toothbrush away.

Now use these pages to make a little book about another activity you do. It might be getting ready for bed, playing a game, or riding your bike. Add words and pictures. Each page should show a different part of the activity. Make sure your pages are in the right order.

Building a Castle

This castle needs three more rows of blocks on the bottom. Cut out as many blocks as you need from the blocks below. Then glue them in place to finish the castle.

Name _____

Busy Day

Mr. Harris has a lot to do. Can you help him? First read the list of things he has to do. Next, look at the map. Number the errands to show the order he should follow to get done very fast. Then draw a line on the map to show his path.

Things to Do

Buy bread and eggs _____

Pick up cleaning _____

Drop off cake at school bakesale _____

Mail letters and buy stamps _____

Return Mr. Robert's wrench _____

Buy food for Sally's frog _____

Leave shoes to be fixed _____

Eat lunch at the diner _____

Name _____

Lunch Time

To make a jelly sandwich you have to do everything in the right order. First think about making a jelly sandwich. Next read all the steps listed below. Cross out two steps you do not need. Then list the steps from 1 to 5 in the order they should be done.

Steps

_____ Eat the sandwich!

_____ Spread the jelly on one piece.

_____ Peel the banana.

_____ Take out the bread and jelly.

_____ Cut the sandwich into pieces.

_____ Take out the apples.

_____ Put the other piece of bread on top.

Write 5 steps in order for one of the following:
○ washing your face
○ preparing a bowl of cereal
○ sending a birthday card to a friend or relative.

Henry and Millie

Henry is coming home from the store. He has eggs, milk, and dog food. He has his dogs Fifi and Princess, too. Millie is coming home from the store, too. She has a birthday cake. She is walking with her cats Bruno and Sam.

Tell what you think will happen next.

_____

_____

_____

_____

_____

_____

_____

Get to Work!

What a mess! It is time to clean up the classroom. Write down all the things that need to be done.

_____

_____

_____

_____

Now you know what to do. But how will you do it? Put all the steps in order to get the job done as fast as you can. Write your answer in the space below. Then change papers with a friend. Tell your friend why you put the steps in the order you did.

_____

_____

_____

_____

Happily Ever After?

Cinderella and the Prince live happily ever after—or do they? Tell what happens to Cinderella and the Prince after they marry. Do they go to school? Get jobs? Have kids? Move to another place? Write on these lines:

_____

_____

_____

_____

_____

_____

And what about Little Red Riding Hood or Snow White and the Seven Dwarves? Pick another fairy tale that you know well. Write what happens after the story ends. Write on these lines:

_____

_____

_____

_____

_____

What If . . .

What do you think would happen if . . .

1. there were no trees? _____

_____

_____

2. people had super-hearing? _____

_____

_____

3. animals could talk? _____

_____

_____

4. there was no night? _____

_____

_____

5. no one had televisions? _____

_____

_____

Picture This!

Look at each picture below. Then underline the sentence that tells what will probably happen next.

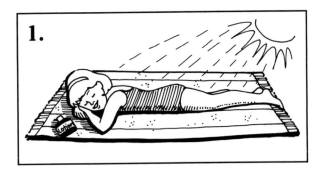

a. A bear borrows the girl's suntan lotion.
b. It begins to snow.
c. The girl gets a sunburn.

a. The boy buys more food because he is still very hungry.
b. The boy gets a stomachache.
c. The boy begins to juggle the food.

a. The girl hits the ball and runs to first base.
b. The girl begins to dance.
c. The girl does a flip.

a. The boy puts the snowball in his pocket to keep it warm.
b. The boy eats the snowball for lunch.
c. The boy throws the snowball at a friend.

Draw a picture of someone in the middle of an activity. Then write three sentences telling what might happen next. Two can be silly, but one must make sense. Then share it with a friend.

Inferring and Drawing Conclusions

From the time they are born, children make inferences about the world in which they live. Through body language, sounds, and visual clues they are able to gather information and reflect on their experience. The activities in this section are designed to strengthen children's critical thinking skills by developing their ability to use multisensory clues to make inferences and draw conclusions.

The activities in this section may be presented on their own or, in many cases, used to complement the various content areas. For example, "Walk This Way" (page 66) works especially well with social studies and map work; and "The Vonce" (page 67) is perfect for units on animals and habitats.

No matter how you choose to use these activities, make sure to give students ample time to form their responses.

What Do I See?

This activity helps develop children's ability to draw inferences from verbal clues. You may wish to use it as a warm-up, as it encourages children to begin thinking about the thinking process itself.

Begin by asking students how they might describe an object—say a blimp or a dragon—to someone who had never seen one before. Would the name of the object alone have any meaning? Why or why not? Explore with children how they might describe the object without naming it.

Have children work with a partner. Ask one partner to make a pair of "binoculars" with his or her hands and to look through them at something they see in the classroom or outside the window. (Suggest that they choose an object that is neither too big nor too small!) Have students give their partners a series of clues that describe the object without naming it. As soon as partners have guessed the identity of the object, have students switch roles and repeat the activity.

After each round, encourage children to discuss how they figured out the mystery. Ask them to describe which clues were most effective and why. Write some of the most successful kinds of clues on the board, such as "Jonah's clue about the size of the object told me it had to be outside the window," or, "Since I knew the object was red, it had to be either Mark's jacket, Cindy's sweater, or the brick building across the street."

Moody Blues

One of the most effective—and fun—ways to develop inferential thinking is through acting. This activity uses pantomime to help children learn to use visual clues in forming inferences.

Explain to children that a mood is a certain way you feel. Invite them to name some moods, such as "sad," "happy," "surprised," "scared," and "angry." Ask students if they have ever known how a friend or family member felt without that person saying a word. Discuss how a person's "body language" and facial expressions are clues to his or her mood. Then tell children that you are going to show them a mood using only your face and body.

Demonstrate an angry mood by standing with folded arms, tightening your shoulders, pressing your lips together, and frowning. Ask children to look at your face and body and suggest words that describe your mood. After children have made their suggestions, encourage them to describe the clues they used to infer your mood.

Continue the activity by asking volunteers to portray other moods. After each round, ask students to discuss the clues they used to infer the mood. You might also want to have students work in pairs and take turns pantomiming and inferring moods.

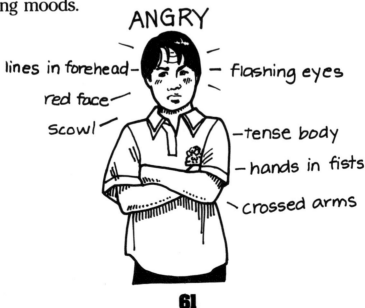

ANGRY

lines in forehead

flashing eyes

red face

scowl

tense body

hands in fists

crossed arms

Definition Derby

In this activity, children infer a word's meaning through the use of context clues. Read the following sentences to children and ask them to define the underlined word. (You might wish to reproduce this page so more assured readers can follow along as you read.) As each word is defined, have children explain how they inferred its meaning. Which clues in each sentence proved to be most helpful?

1. The *ancient* building was built a long, long time ago.

2. Have they *captured* the tiger that escaped from the zoo?

3. How did Marc *reply* to the question?

4. You can cut your lip on a broken cup *rim*.

5. The clown made Maria feel more *cheerful*.

6. It was *damp* outside after the rain.

7. The light was so *faint* I could hardly see it.

8. Luke could not drink the milk because it was *spoiled*.

9. Chris *seized* the toy from his sister.

10. They *chatted* so much that their teacher had to tell them to keep quiet.

11. Henry tried to *conceal* his braces by closing his mouth.

12. The room was *vacant* after all the children left.

13. Mrs. Smith tried to *coax* her daughter into drinking her milk.

14. The teacher asked Charles to *fetch* the books from the cupboard.

15. Kids *loathe* liver and spinach.

16. The *agile* tumbler could touch her nose to her knees.

17. D.J. wanted to *assemble* the kit on his own.

Definition Derby
(continued)

18. Because they were not in a hurry, the kids *ambled* home slowly after school.

19. The sponge was so *moist* that it was dripping.

20. The space between the earth and the sun is very *vast*.

21. The wrecking crane was set to *demolish* the office.

22. My mother's fingers are so *nimble* that she can untie any knot.

23. Put a sweater on because it is *chilly* tonight.

24. The *flexible* tube bent easily.

25. The child's hands were *grimy* after he played in the dirt.

Mystery Box

This activity encourages students to examine and interpret information and then apply their knowledge to new situations.

Before class begins, make a collection of familiar objects, such as buttons, coins, and crayons. Select one object and place it in a covered shoe box. To begin the activity, tell students you have placed an object in the box. Explain that you are going to write the names of five objects on the board, and that one of the objects will be the one in the box. For beginning students, you may wish to list objects that are very different; for more advanced students, you may want to list objects that are similar.

Then invite students to guess what is in the box by asking you *yes* and *no* questions. For example, they might ask, "Is the item metal?" "Do you cut with it?" "Can I buy things with it?" Encourage students to base each successive question on the information they have gleaned from the previous question, and to use the information to eliminate possibilities. Repeat the activity several times, using a different object each time. With each round, challenge students to guess the object using fewer and fewer questions.

As children become more familiar with the activity, you may wish to have them do the activity in small groups, with one person in each group serving as the leader. The first student to guess the object in the box becomes the group's next leader.

Short Stuff

Juan is taller than Malcolm but shorter than Hong.

Answer these questions:

1. Who is the shortest? _____

2. Who is in the middle? _____

3. Who is the tallest? _____

Cathy is shorter than Lynn but taller than Shaketa.

Answer these questions:

1. Who is the shortest? _____

2. Who is in the middle? _____

3. Who is the tallest? _____

Name _____

Walk This Way

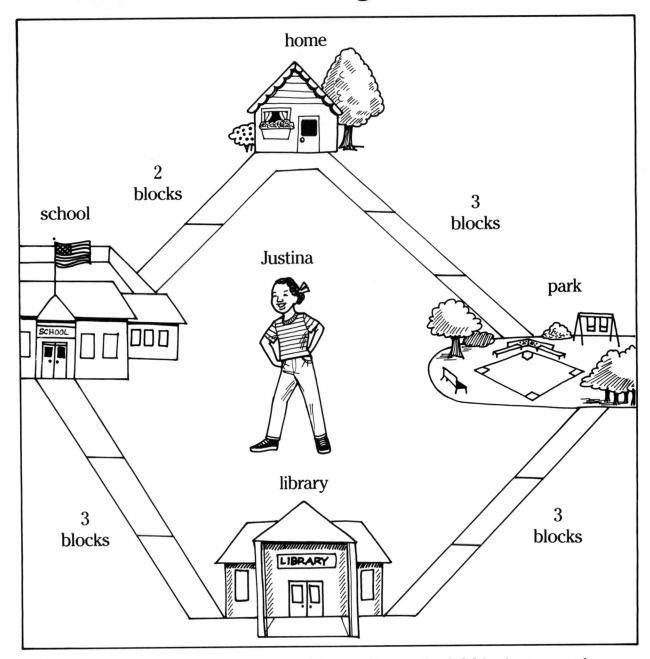

Justina walked from her home to the library. She walked 6 blocks to get there. She rested when she was halfway there. Where do you think she rested?

_____

How do you know? _____

The Vonce

Here's a Vonce. It is a make-believe animal. The Vonce has two short front legs. Its front feet have sharp claws. Its back feet are webbed. Its tail is short and furry. Its body has thick fur. The fur is brown in the summer and white in the winter. The Vonce has big, round ears. It has a long nose. Its eyes are very small. Its teeth are very sharp.

What can you tell about the Vonce by the way it looks?

1. Do you think it is cold where the Vonce lives? _____

Explain your answer. _____

2. Do you think the Vonce can swim? _____

Explain your answer. _____

3. Do you think the Vonce can climb trees? _____

Why or why not? _____

4. Do you think the Vonce can hear well? _____

Explain your answer. _____

5. Do you think the Vonce can run fast? _____

Explain your answer. _____

Too Many Facts?

These children want to do something. But before they can do it, they need to know some facts. Cross out the fact that will *not* help them.

1. Chris is going to call a friend. She needs to know:
   a. her friend's phone number
   b. her friend's address
   c. how to dial the phone

2. Tammi is going to play soccer. She needs to know:
   a. where the game is
   b. what clothing to wear
   c. who built the field

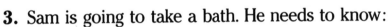

3. Sam is going to take a bath. He needs to know:
   a. how to turn the water on
   b. where his boots are
   c. where the soap is

4. Jim is getting ready for school. He needs to know:
   a. what's for dinner
   b. if it is a rainy day
   c. what time it is

Try This

Write a problem like one of the ones above. Include two facts that are needed and one that isn't. Trade papers with a classmate.

Name _____

Close It Up!

Read the words.

rat	The rat runs.	*fat*	The rat is fat.
cat	The cat runs.	*did*	The rat did run.
see	I see the rat.	*and*	The rat and cat run.
for	Look for the cat!	*you*	Did you look for me?

Write in the missing word.

1. _____ you see
the cat?

Did   For

5. I _____ the cat.

     see   fat

2. The cat is _____!

for   fat

6. You can see the _____.

     rat   and

3. The cat looks _____
the rat.

you   for

7. Did _____ see
the rat?

     fat   you

4. You _____ the cat
did run.

and   fat

8. The _____ did go.

     you   cat

Name _____

Why?

Some strange things have happened. Write a sentence to explain what could have made each of these things happen.

1. All the lights have gone off. _____

_____

_____

2. The leaves did not fall off the trees. _____

_____

_____

3. Golden snowflakes are falling from the sky. _____

_____

_____

4. Everyone has green hair. _____

_____

_____

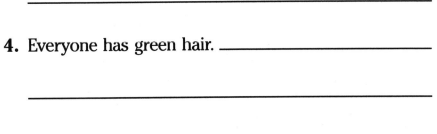

5. Animals can talk. _____

_____

_____

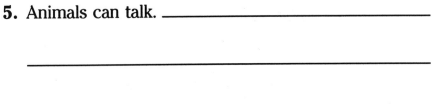

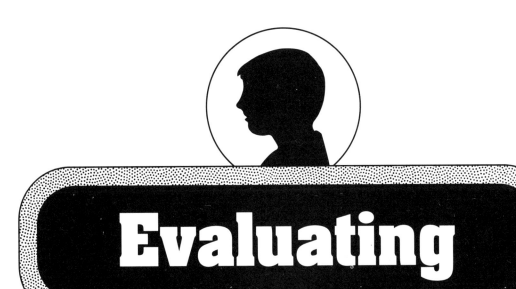

Evaluating

Before children start this section, explain to them that *evaluating* means making a judgment about something. Point out to students that they make many evaluations during the day—evaluations about people, events, things they see, things they eat, and things they read. Ask children to mention one thing they have made an evaluation about that day.

Each of the following ten activities guides students through the process of evaluating different kinds of things. In "Yummy, Yummy, In My Tummy" (page 78) and "Good For Your Teeth!" (page 80), for example, children will be evaluating food. "Pet Shopping" (page 79) and "Meow!" (page 83) focus on evaluating animals and people; "The Better Buy" (page 82) and "Buy This A" (page 77) provide training in evaluating the value of objects. You can present each of these activities as a discrete lesson or integrate them into a specific content area.

Pitch In!

This activity is designed to help children evaluate how their time and energy can best be applied to conserving wildlife and protecting the environment. After they have completed their evaluation, children can create and implement a plan suited to their abilities and goals.

Begin by exploring with children some of the different things they can do—both as individuals and in small groups—to help the environment. They may suggest picking up garbage, recycling plastic and glass, feeding wild creatures in the winter, avoiding the use of aerosol sprays.

Next, divide the class into small groups. Have each group formulate a simple, workable plan to help preserve the environment. Suggest that students first establish realistic goals. Ask them if they wish to work in their homes, at school, or through the local park, for instance. Do they think they should join an established school or community group, or would they be better off working on their own? Ask each group to present its plan to the class in the form of a panel discussion. Then have the class vote on the plan they think will be the most successful. Finally, have students as a class implement the plan they have chosen.

As students work, they might want to contact the following agencies for suggestions and resources:

Center for Environmental Information, Inc.
99 Court Street, Rochester, NY 14604/(716) 546-3796

CEI is a nonprofit organization that provides materials concerning environmental and conservation issues. Information is free.

Pitch In! (continued)

Children of the Green Earth
307 N. 48th, Seattle, WA 98103/(206) 781-0852

CGE, a nonprofit organization, encourages students to "regreen" the earth by planting trees and caring for forests.

The Cousteau Society
930 W. 21st Street, Norfolk, VA 23517/(804) 627-1144

The Cousteau Society runs a number of programs and disseminates information on environmental issues. Dolphin Log is a bimonthly magazine with stories, games, facts, and experiments for children ages seven and up.

Earth Island Institute
300 Broadway, Suite 28, San Francisco, CA 94133/
(415) 788-3666

This nonprofit organization develops and supports innovative activities to restore and preserve the environment.

Kids Against Pollution
PO Box 775, Closter, NJ 07624/(201) 784-0668

Created by a group of elementary school children from New Jersey, KAP is an excellent source of information on what children can do in their schools, homes, and communities to help the environment. Yearly membership is $6.00.

National Recycling Coalition, Inc.
1101 30th Street, NW, Suite 305, Washington, DC 20007/
(202) 625-6406

NRC, a nonprofit organization, runs a number of programs, including Peer Match, which provides assistance to communities wishing to implement recycling programs.

Everyone's a Critic

Ask students to brainstorm a list of television shows that they watch. Write the list on the board and have children vote for their three favorite shows. Then ask children to explain why they voted as they did. What makes this television show enjoyable? Is it the characters? The situations? Maybe the music? What are the factors that make a television show good or bad?

Help children count the votes and write the names of the three winning shows on the board. Then ask children to watch the shows during the week. Have children answer these questions in writing:

○ What is the name of the show?
○ Name three things you liked in this episode.
○ Name three things you did not like in this episode.
○ Rank the three shows in the order that you liked them. Write one sentence explaining why you ranked the shows as you did.

Invite students to discuss their evaluations in class, focusing on the critical factors that were most important to them.

You may wish to conclude the activity by challenging children to design their own television shows based on the qualities of the shows they ranked the highest. Have them work in small groups to create characters and situations that have meaning and impact, and to suggest appropriate music. Invite them to perform brief skits from their shows for the class.

The Sky Is Falling!

A good way to develop children's ability to evaluate is through a literature-based approach. Obtain a version of "Chicken Little" or "The Three Sillies," both of which are folktales about characters who draw absurd conclusions from scant evidence. Read one or both of the stories to the class. Then lead a class discussion focusing on the following questions:

○ What did the characters believe would happen?
○ What evidence did they have?
○ Was it enough evidence?
○ How else might they have interpreted the situation?
○ What else might they have done? What would you have done?
○ Do you think the way they acted was silly? Why or why not?
○ What did the characters' behavior tell you about them?

Then challenge students to come up with their own "folktales" based on characters who jump to conclusions without carefully evaluating the evidence. Have children work in small groups to brainstorm their folktale ideas. If you wish, allow them to perform their stories as skits.

Class Flag

Guide students to brainstorm a list of important items in the classroom. For example, children might suggest the fish tank, the guinea pigs, the easels, the reading corner, the science corner, the rug, the desks, the alphabet chart, or the terrarium. Then have children suggest ideas that are important in the classroom, such as cooperation, sharing, and encouragement. Write all the ideas on the board as children suggest them.

Explain to students that they are going to make a class flag. Point out that the colors and designs on a flag usually tell something about the nation or organization represented by the flag. Ask students if they know what the stars and stripes and the red, white, and blue colors on the American flag mean. Invite students to mention other flags they may be familiar with and ask volunteers to talk about flags they may have made in organizations such as the 4-H or the Scouts.

Suggest to students that their class flag tell something about what their class is like and what makes it special. Divide the class into small groups and have children look at the items on the board—adding any additional ones they want—and then create a design for a flag using any of the items. Encourage children to work cooperatively to design and color their flag.

When everyone is finished, have each group display its flag and explain what each of the items represents. Children may also wish to write brief descriptions of their flags. Display the flags in a prominent place so everyone can enjoy them.

Buy This A!

Another way to help children develop their evaluation skills is to have them create their own commercials. Rather than asking them to sell a product, however, this activity asks them to sell letters of the alphabet.

Start by leading a discussion focusing on familiar commercials such as those for toys or food items. Ask students to name the commercials they like best and to tell why they like them. Point out that commercials often make one product seem better than another even though the products may be very similar. Explore the various ways advertisers make an item seem attractive, for example, by stressing its usefulness, appearance, or rarity. Tell children that they will now get a chance to advertise something that is *really* worthwhile—the letters of the alphabet!

Arrange children in pairs. Explain that their task is to sell a letter of the alphabet in a brief "television commercial." Assign each team a letter of the alphabet, including both common letters, such as *a, e,* and *s,* and less-common letters, such as *x, z,* and *q.* Have each group begin by thinking of ways their letter might be attractive to others. Does it have special uses? What words can it create? In what ways does it look pretty or special? Is it valuable because it is rare?

When everyone is finished, have each team present its commercial to the class. To summarize, have children decide which letters they might want to buy. Encourage them to cite specific reasons for their decision.

Name _____

Yummy, Yummy in My Tummy

Think about what you ate yesterday. Make a list of the foods you ate at each meal. If you liked the food a lot, write a 1 next to it. If you liked it a little, write a 2 next to it. If you didn't like it at all, write a 3 next to it. At the end, tell which food was your favorite.

Breakfast   #   Lunch   #

_____   ___   _____   ___

_____   ___   _____   ___

_____   ___   _____   ___

_____   ___   _____   ___

Dinner   #   Snacks   #

_____   ___   _____   ___

_____   ___   _____   ___

_____   ___   _____   ___

_____   ___   _____   ___

My favorite food of all was _____

Pet Shopping

What kinds of animals would you like to have as pets? Beside each animal, list some things that make it a good pet. Then list some things that might make it not such a good pet.

	Good Pet:	**Not a Good Pet:**
	_____	_____
	_____	_____
	_____	_____
	_____	_____
	_____	_____
	_____	_____
	_____	_____
	_____	_____
	_____	_____
	_____	_____

Which pet would you like to have? _____

Write two sentences to explain why. _____

_____

_____

_____

_____

Good for Your Teeth!

You probably know that sugar can cause cavities. Sugar is found in foods that are very sweet. Look at the list below. Cross out the foods that are not good for your teeth.

What foods *are* good for your teeth? Draw some of them here.

The Perfect Day

There are a lot of things you can do in a day. Here are some things to do. Are there others? Write them on the lines. Next circle five of the things you did this week. List them in order on the chart—from your most favorite to your least favorite.

reading

sleeping

writing

eating

cleaning your room

watching tv

playing with friends

going to school

taking a bath

_____   _____   _____

Most favorite   Least favorite

What is the thing you like to do the most? _____

Write a sentence to tell why. _____

_____

Name _____

The Better Buy

Bigger can be better—but not all the time! Decide which item is a better buy. Then tell why on the lines below.

1. The small box of soap is $1.   The big box is $2.

The Joneses have three children. Which box of soap is a better buy for the

family? _____

Why? _____

2. The small milk costs 25¢.   The large milk costs $1.

Juan lives alone and eats out a lot. Which milk should he buy? _____

Why? _____

3. One puppy costs $5.   Six puppies cost $20.

The Bengels live in an apartment and have a cat. Should they buy one puppy

or six? _____

Why? _____

Name _____

Meow!

Think about what you know about cats. People and cats are the same in some ways, but not in other ways. Write words that describe people in the People circle. Write words that describe cats in the Cats circle. Write words that describe <u>both</u> people and cats in the space where the circles overlap.

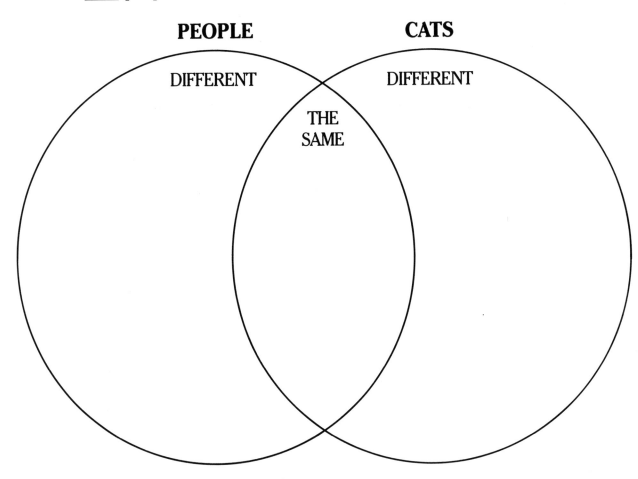

PEOPLE   **CATS**

DIFFERENT   DIFFERENT

THE
SAME

Look back at the circles. Do you think people and cats are more like each other

or more not like each other? _____

Why? _____

_____

_____

Name _____

Thumbs Up,
Thumbs Down

Pick a book you read a short time ago.
Tell what you think about it by answering
these questions:

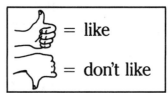
= like

= don't like

1. What is the title? _____

2. Who is the author? _____

CIRCLE ONE

3. Did you like the way the book started?

   Write a sentence to explain your answer. _____

   _____

4. Did you like the people or animals in the story?

   Write a sentence to explain your answer. _____

   _____

5. Did you like the pictures in the story?

   Write a sentence to explain your answer. _____

   _____

6. Did you like the ending of the story?

   Write a sentence to explain your answer. _____

   _____

7. Would you tell a friend to read this story?

   Write a sentence to explain your answer. _____

   _____

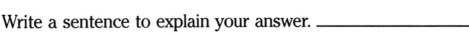

Analyzing

Ask children if they have ever been faced with a really tricky problem—something they couldn't solve in an instant. It might have been a problem in math, or a problem finding a lost item, or a problem deciding how to make the best use of their time.

Point out to children that no matter what the problem, a good way to solve it is to *analyze* it. Explain that analyzing a problem means breaking the problem down into smaller parts or "steps" and then thinking about each step on its own. Tell students that when they analyze a problem in this way, they are better able to predict possible outcomes and propose solutions that make sense.

After you have discussed this process, you may wish to model it by working through some of the activities in this section. Consider using "Grog Is Rich!" (page 89) or "Big Sale!" (page 90). Think aloud as you work in order to demonstrate your thinking process to your students. As you work, encourage students to be participants in the process. After you have finished modeling the activity, ask children to comment on the way you arrived at your solution.

Guess the Rule

The object of this game is for children to use analysis to figure out a rule. Tell children that you are going to think of a rule and then challenge them to guess what it is. Explain that you will tell them only which of them fits the rule and which of them don't.

Seat children in a circle. Think of a simple rule, such as *you must wear the color red,* or *you must wear a t-shirt with writing on it.* Working around the circle, tell children whether they fit the rule or not. Have children who fit the rule take a place in the center of the circle. Instruct the rest of the class to analyze the children in the circle to see what they might have in common.

As soon as someone thinks they know the rule, ask them for the name of another student who fits the rule. If the child answers correctly, ask him or her to state the rule. The child who guesses correctly can think of a new rule for the next round.

What do these children have in common?

(They are all wearing high-top sneakers.)

What Should We Do?

Present each of the following situations to the entire class, or have students work in small groups. Ask students to analyze each situation and then present their solutions. Discuss each analysis with students.

1. Two friends want to play with the same toy. How can they solve their problems without fighting?

2. If you lost your mittens, how could you keep your hands warm?

3. How many ways can you melt an ice cube?

4. What is the sun good for?

5. If you were outside and it began to rain, what would you do to keep dry?

6. What would you do if your bed disappeared?

7. What would you do if you could be invisible that you would otherwise not do?

8. How many things can you do with snow?

9. How many ways can you get balls down from the school roof?

10. How could you wash the outside of these windows from the inside?

Mystery Word

Analyzing words for specific sounds helps children develop both analyzing and decoding skills. Begin this activity by telling children that you are going to name a group of things and read some words that belong to that group. Write the following groups on the board: *people, vegetables, body parts, colors, clothing,* and *bugs.* Challenge students to identify the mystery word in each group. The mystery word is the word with the /ē/ sound as in *bee* and *seat.*

For each category, slowly read each of the words below and direct children to write the word with the /ē/ sound in their notebooks:

People: you, us, we, them (we)

Vegetables: lettuce, beans, carrots, corn (beans)

Body parts: hands, toes, nose, feet (feet)

Colors: red, blue, yellow, green (green)

Clothing: hat, shoes, jeans, shirt, (jeans)

Bugs: fly, spider, ant, bee, (bee)

Continue the same activity with the short /a/ sound as in *nap.*

People: girl, Bill, man, they (man)

Vegetables: peas, potatoes, carrots, tomatoes (carrots)

Body Parts: hand, brain, knee, neck (hand)

Colors: pink, orange, black, white (black)

Clothing: coat, mittens, hat, sweater (hat)

Bugs: butterfly, worm, grasshopper, bee (grasshopper)

You can use this activity to help children analyze any sound you are reviewing or introducing.

Grog Is Rich!

Grog is a caveman. He uses shells for money. This is what his money is worth:

 Conch shells are each worth 2 cents.

 Clams are each worth 4 cents.

Shiny shells each are worth 6 cents.

How much money does Grog have? Write your answers on the lines.

1. 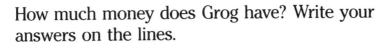 _____ cents

2. _____ cents

3. _____ cents

4. _____ cents

5. How much money does Grog have altogether? _____ cents

Draw a money problem like the one above in the box below. Then ask a classmate to tell you how much money Grog has.

Name _____

Big Sale!

How much can you buy at the big sale? Answer the questions to find out!

3 bears cost 15¢

1 bear and
2 robots cost 19¢

2 bears and
1 robot cost 17¢

How much does a bear cost? _____

How much does a robot cost? _____

If you had 10¢, what would you buy? _____

3 balls cost 9¢

2 balls and
1 game cost 16¢

1 ball and
2 games cost 23¢

How much does a ball cost? _____

How much does a game cost? _____

If you had 13¢, what would you buy? _____

Name _____

Unlock the Mystery

A big jewelry robbery! Officer Perez knows the robber hid the jewels in one of these bank boxes. She has three clues:

1. The box number is greater than 7.

2. The box number is less than 10.

3. You *don't* say the box number when you count by twos.

Which box holds the jewels? Write your answer on this line: _____

Then tell how you figured out the answer: _____

_____

_____

_____

Pick a Winner

Read each sentence. Pick the word you think best answers the question.

1. Which is the best pet?	tiger	bear	bird	moth
2. What keeps you warm?	milk	pen	coat	tree
3. Which is fastest?	fish in bowl	turtle	car	plane
4. Which is coldest?	ice	carrots	dog's nose	pea
5. Which is slowest?	bird	worm	jet	train
6. Which is nearest?	star	ground	clouds	sun
7. Which is deepest?	pond	puddle	ocean	tub
8. Which is brightest?	lamp	sun	electric eel	moon
9. Which is biggest?	banana	ear	dime	toe
10. Which is the softest?	hill	pillow	ice	rock

Sit with a friend. Talk about your answers. Explain why you chose your answers.

Write four possible answers for each of these questions. Make sure only one of the answers is correct: *Which is lightest? Which is tallest? Which is hottest?* Then give the questions to a classmate and ask him or her to circle the correct choice.

Clowning Around

This clown needs help! He is too busy clowning around to color in his bowling pins. Read the clues and color in the pins for the clown. Then color in the clown.

Clues

1. One of the pins is orange.

2. The red pin is highest.

3. The green pin is nearest to the ground.

4. The yellow pin is by his nose.

5. The blue pin is between the yellow one and the green one.

What's That Again?

The sentences below do not make sense. Read them
and you will see! Look at the underlined word.
Change the word so the sentence makes sense!

1. In the spring, the <u>birds</u> get leaves. _____

2. The dog chewed on the <u>saw</u>. _____

3. I ate my soup with a <u>pen</u>. _____

4. After it snows we make a <u>mail</u>man. _____

5. I was cold so I put on a <u>nose</u>. _____

6. Cats love to catch <u>doors</u>. _____

7. I used a <u>hat</u> to sweep the floor. _____

8. It is fun to swim in <u>ears</u>. _____

9. Brush your <u>toes</u> before you go to sleep. _____

10. Write your words with a <u>pickle</u>. _____

Now, write three sentences like the ones you just read. Use one word that does
not fit and underline it. Share your sentences with a friend.

1. _____

2. _____

3. _____

Same Things?

Each line has two words. Read the two words and see if they have the same meaning. If they mean the same thing, circle *same*. If they do not mean the same thing, circle *not the same*.

1. big	**small**	same	not the same
2. sad	**happy**	same	not the same
3. dog	**cat**	same	not the same
4. neat	**messy**	same	not the same
5. buddy	**pal**	same	not the same
6. fire	**ice**	same	not the same
7. sun	**moon**	same	not the same
8. make	**build**	same	not the same
9. eat	**sleep**	same	not the same
10. right	**left**	same	not the same
11. cry	**sob**	same	not the same
12. see	**look**	same	not the same

Pick any five examples where the words do not mean the same thing. Write down each pair of words and explain why they are not the same. Use these lines:

Words: **Why they are not the same:**

1. _____   _____

2. _____   _____

3. _____   _____

4. _____   _____

5. _____   _____

If I Were a...

If you were a bird, what kind would you be? If you were a color, what color would you be? Let's find out!

1. If I were a bird, I would be a _____

because _____

_____

2. If I were a color, I would be the color _____

because _____

_____

3. If I were a place, I would be _____

because _____

_____

4. If I were a tree, I would be a _____

because _____

_____

5. If I were a tool, I would be a _____

because _____

_____

Synthesizing

Explain to children that *synthesizing* means "putting it all together." Tell students that in this section they will get a chance to put together information they already know to figure out new things. "Voom Voom Vehicle" (page 99), for example, challenges students to use all of the critical thinking skills they have learned so far to build a class vehicle. In "Use It!" (page 105), students create new uses for familiar objects and figure out what purposes unfamiliar objects might serve. Encourage children to take their time and think carefully as they work through the final section of the book.

You might want to encourage children to work together in small groups. Make sure everyone in the group has a specific task to perform—one that is suited to their skills, strengths, and interests. Such activities as "Games Galore" (page 98), "Rain, Rain, Come Today" (page 102), and "What a Machine!" (page 106) lend themselves well to this approach.

Games Galore

This activity helps children develop their synthesizing skills by challenging them to create an original game from an assortment of commonplace materials. Before class, fill seven or eight large-sized envelopes with an assortment of the following materials:

○ straws   ○ gum balls   ○ rubber bands
○ paper clips   ○ index cards   ○ safety pins
○ paper tubes   ○ spools   ○ buttons

Vary the contents of each envelope slightly.

When class begins, assemble children into groups of three to five members and give each an envelope of materials. Explain to students that they are to use the materials in the envelope to invent their own game. Their game may have a board, but it does not have to. They do not have to use all the materials in the envelope, nor do they have to use them in their current form. The paper clip, for example, can be stretched out, and the paper tube can be cut or unwound. They can use an index card to jot down the rules of their game, if they wish. Give children ample time to invent their games.

Have each group share its game by showing how it is played.

Voom Voom Vehicle

Read Gail Gibbons' book *Trucks* (HarperCollins) to the class. Discuss with children the vehicles mentioned in the book and how they function. Then tell students that in this activity they will have a chance to build their own vehicles and explain what they can do.

Obtain half a dozen large cardboard boxes from a supermarket. Ask students to bring from home any discarded containers, such as paper towel and toilet paper tubes and shoe and gift boxes. Have small groups of students use the available materials to create their vehicles. Students may paint, color, and decorate their vehicles. Aluminum foil works especially well for decorating. After all groups have completed their vehicles, ask each group to name its vehicle and then to explain how it functions, how it can be used, and any special features it may have.

Fishy Stuff

This two-part activity draws together the various critical thinking skills children have learned thus far, focusing on synthesis. You can use this activity on its own, or in conjunction with a science lesson.

Children as Authors

To begin, read children a story that involves characters and salty ocean water or fresh lake water. For example, Syd Hoff's *Sammy the Seal* (HarperCollins) is a good choice for beginning learners. Explore how different animals need salt or fresh water to survive. Ask children which kind of water humans need.

Then have children create individual books about creatures that live in either fresh water or salt water. Begin by brainstorming a list of creatures that live in the ocean, such as whales, dolphins, lobsters, tuna, crabs, starfish, and seals. Then create a list of creatures that live in fresh water, such as salmon, turtles, frogs, and goldfish. Invite children to select one of these creatures as the subject for a story, and allow time for writing. When children have finished writing, have them copy their stories onto sheets of unlined paper folded down the middle and stapled in place. Suggest that children illustrate each page of text and create a cover for their books. When the books are complete, display them on a shelf or table and allow students to peruse each others' writing at their leisure.

Fishy Stuff (continued)

Hands On! Experiment

Here's a way to help children explore the difference between fresh and salt water first-hand. You will need two small paper cups for each child, water, and some table salt.

Start by asking children to recall some ways that lakes are different from oceans. Write students' responses on the board, encouraging them to infer differences from the size and location of the oceans and lakes as well as the creatures that live in each. Remind students that rivers are made of fresh water—water without salt—and oceans are made of salt water. In addition, remind students that some creatures can only live in salt water; some creatures can only live in fresh water.

To help children understand the difference between river water and ocean water, conduct the following experiment. Have student volunteers distribute two cups partly filled with water to each student. Ask children how they might learn more about the water they have. They might suggest tasting it, smelling it, and touching it, for example. Then ask students to add about a teaspoon of salt to one of their cups and to stir the water with a finger until the salt dissolves. Have students decide how the salty water is different from the fresh water. Does it taste different? Does it look or smell different? Lastly, ask students to discuss how they reached their conclusions. What thinking skills did they use?

Children might also enjoy recalling some of the creatures that can live in only salt water and those that can only live in fresh water.

Rain, Rain, Come Today!

This activity uses science concepts to help children strengthen their synthesizing skills.

Begin by explaining that all living things need water, and that it is important for regions to get enough rain. Then ask children if they know a way to measure rainfall. Solicit students' ideas and record them on the board. After exploring each idea, explain that one way people can measure rainfall is with a rain gauge. Tell them that in this activity they will make a gauge to measure rainfall.

Divide the class into small groups. Give each group a wide-mouthed plastic jar with straight sides, a millimeter ruler, and a piece of tape. Ask them to tape the ruler against the side of the jar, with the bottom of the ruler level with the bottom of the jar.

When each group is finished making its rain gauge, have students place the gauges outside in an open area. Ask them to predict how much rain they think they will collect during an average rainstorm. After a rainstorm has occurred, have children bring their gauges indoors. Help them to read the ruler to measure how much rain has fallen. Record the measurements on a class chart. Repeat this procedure until the class collects data from several rainstorms. Ask students: Do you think these numbers will be the same for every rainfall? For every season? In every region of the country?

Then have the class explore what they learned from this experiment. Ask students what critical thinking skills they think they used. Guide them to see how they recalled what they knew about rain, visualized how plants get water, followed directions to make the gauge, predicted rainfall, analyzed data, and synthesized their findings.

Paint a Rainbow

All colors can be made with red, blue, and yellow. Follow the color chart and use red, blue, and yellow paint to make all the colors of the rainbow. Then use the colors you made to fill in the rainbow below.

Color Chart

purple = red + blue

green = yellow + blue

orange = red + yellow

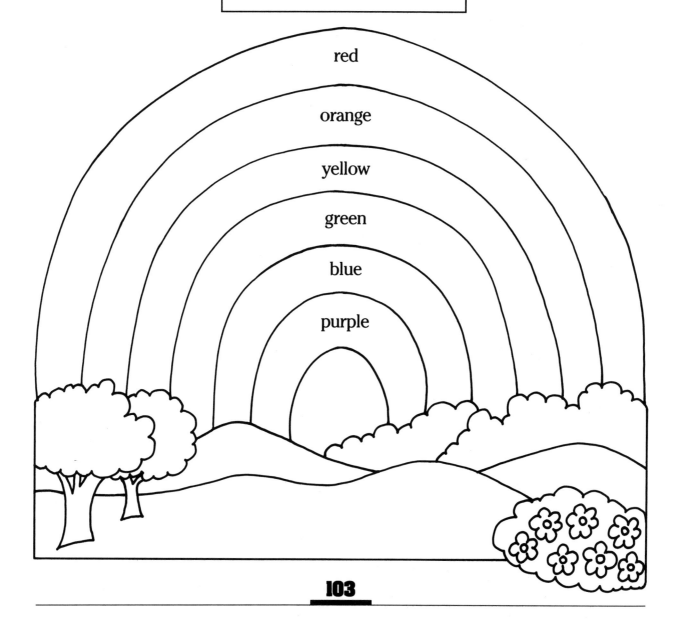

red

orange

yellow

green

blue

purple

Name _____

Three Wishes

You have been given three wishes. What will you wish for?

Wish 1 _____

_____

Tell why you made this wish. _____

_____

Wish 2 _____

_____

Tell why you made this wish. _____

_____

Wish 3 _____

_____

Tell why you made this wish. _____

_____

Pick any one wish. Explain how your life would be different if the wish came

true. _____

_____

Use It!

How many new ways can you use this comb? List the ways here:

_____

_____

_____

_____

_____

How many ways can you use this pot? List the ways here:

_____

_____

_____

_____

_____

List five new ways to use this eraser. List the ways here:

_____

_____

_____

_____

_____

How many new ways can you use this toothbrush? List the ways here:

_____

_____

_____

_____

_____

What a Machine!

Machines help us do things faster and better. What do these machines help us do? Write a sentence telling what each helps us do.

_____

_____

_____

_____

_____

What would you like to do faster or better? Invent an item to do it! Draw a picture of your invention in the box.

Write a sentence that tells what it can do. _____

_____

Box It

Cut out these eight shapes.

Make something with them!

You can use all the shapes or just some of them. You can write on the shapes and color them, too. What can you make?

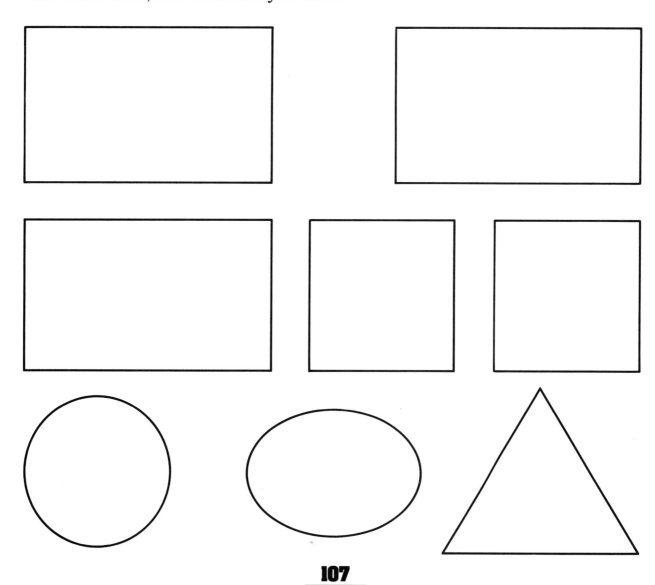

Special Delivery

We write letters to people. They write letters to us. But not all letters are for

people. Write a letter that can't be sent! You can write to an object  ,

nature  , a part of your body  , or someone in a

book .

Write your letter here:

Date _____

Dear _____ ,

_____

_____

_____

_____

_____

_____

_____

Very truly yours,

_____

Answer Key

Answers

Recognizing and Recalling

Home Sweet Home (page 13)
Possible responses:

hive: bee (honey)
nest: birds (worms, bugs)
cave: bear (fruits)
lake: fish, ducks, geese, turtles, frogs (bugs)
tree: squirrels, birds (nuts, bugs)
barn: pigs, chickens, horses (hay, meal)

Snapdragon! (page 18)
Possible responses:

box 1	box 2
daylight	nobody
football	everyone
myself	however
outside	suntan
sometime	handball

box 3	box 4
ice cube	rainbow
inside	pinecone
somebody	penpal
no one	sunlight
sunburn	everybody

A is for. . . (page 20)
Possible responses:

A is for apples
B is for bananas
C is for carrots
D is for dandelions
E is for eggplants
F is for flowers
G is for grapes
H is for hay
I is for irises
J is for junipers
K is for kiwi
L is for lettuce
M is for mint
N is for strawberries
O is for onions
P or Q is for peaches
R is for raspberries
S is for strawberries
T is for tomatoes
U or V is for vanilla
W is for watermelons
X, Y, or Z is for zebras

Distinguishing and Visualizing

Break-Aparts (page 25)
1. I like dogs.
2. We have a dog.
3. He is big.
4. Do you like dogs?
5. This is a busy day.
6. Eat all your lunch.
7. Save me a seat.
8. Where is your house?
9. Do you like to swim?
10. We swim in a lake.
11. The lake is cold.
12. I swim very fast.
13. In winter I skate.
14. The lake is frozen.

Color My World (page 26)

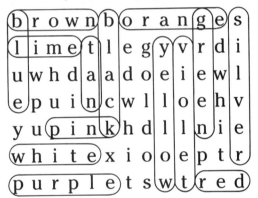

What's Going on Here? (page 27)
Twelve things wrong with the picture:
bathtub, cactus, camel, duck on bike, frog in boots, palm tree, penguin, rabbit with glasses, refrigerator, table, turtle on roller skates, whale.

Near Match (page 28)

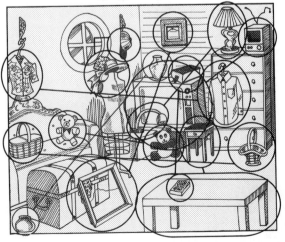

Small, Smaller, Smallest (page 29)

	smallest	largest
1.	pin	bed
2.	grape	truck
3.	snowflake	bridge
4.	ice cube	car
5.	fly	house
6.	cup	ocean
7.	frog	elephant
8.	bee	deer
9.	rose	sun
10.	bean	airplane

It's Handy! (page 30)

1. bigger
2. smaller
3. smaller
4. bigger
5. smaller
6. smaller
7. bigger
8. smaller
9. bigger
10. smaller

Following Directions and Classifying

Clean-Up Time (page 42)
Possible responses:

inside clothing		outside clothing	
slippers	pants	coat	mittens
shoes	pajamas	boots	hat
shirt	robe	scarf	
	socks		

Where Can You Find It? (page 43)
Possible responses:
Park: slide, swing, tree, duck, flower, grass, pond, squirrel, bird, dog, bug, kite, ball, mud, picnic
School: paper, clock, pen, pencil, desk, trash can, note pad, book, ball, lunchroom, crayons
Both places: trash can, slide, swing, ball

Cross It Out! (page 44)
Possible responses:
1. nurse; family members
2. ice; clothing
3. paint; colors
4. pen; parts of body
5. cloud; things that grow
6. book; things you write with
7. summer; precipitation/weather
8. sled; animals
9. peach; vegetables
10. good; things we do
11. green; things that start with O
12. worm; insects
13. steam; frozen water
14. desert; bodies of water
15. ball; flat objects

Great Groups (page 45)
Possible responses:
1. at the beach (cross out sled)
2. in a toolbox (cross out pitcher)
3. in your class (cross out snowman)
4. in a closet (cross out bathtub)
5. in a kitchen (cross out lion)
6. in an office (cross out clown)

What Is What? (page 46)
box 1: The car and boat are vehicles.
box 2: The first and last creatures are zorks.
box 3: The first and second shapes are tombats.
box 4: The first figure is a lork.

Sequencing and Predicting

Brush Your Teeth (page 50)
Correct sequence: Get your toothbrush and toothpaste; squeeze toothpaste onto the brush; put the brush inside your mouth; brush your teeth; rinse your mouth with water; put the toothbrush away.

Building a Castle (page 51)
21 blocks are needed

Busy Day (page 52)

buy bread and eggs	5
Pick up cleaning	4
Drop off cake at school bakesale	6
Mail letters and buy stamps	8
Return Mr. Robert's wrench	3
Buy food for Sally's frog	2
Leave shoes to be fixed	1
Eat lunch at the diner	7

Lunch Time (page 53)
1. Take out the bread and jelly.
2. Spread the jelly on one piece.
3. Put the other piece of bread on top.
4. Cut the sandwich into pieces.
5. Eat the sandwich!

Picture This! (page 58)
1. c. 2. b. 3. a. 4. c.

Inferring and Drawing Conclusions
Short Stuff (page 65)
1. Malcolm is the shortest; Juan is in the middle; Hong is the tallest.
2. Shaketa is the shortest; Cathy is in the middle; Lynn is the tallest.

Walk This Way (page 66)
Possible response:
She stopped at the park. I know because since she walked six blocks, she had to go past the park. The other way is five blocks. The park is halfway to the library.

The Vonce (page 67)
Possible responses:
1. Yes, because the Vonce has a fur coat.
2. The Vonce can swim because it has webbed back feet.
3. Yes, because it has claws on its front feet.
4. Yes, because it has big, round ears.
5. The Vonce would not be a good runner because its front legs are short and have sharp claws. The claws might get caught on the ground.

Too Many Facts? (page 68)
1. b 2. c 3. b 4. a

Close It Up! (page 69)
1. Did   5. see
2. fat   6. rat
3. for   7. you
4. and   8. cat

Evaluating
Good For Your Teeth! (page 80)
Foods that are not good for your teeth include: lollipop, cupcakes, cookies, cola, ice cream sundae.

The Better Buy (page 82)
Possible responses:
1. The big box is a better buy because the Jones family is getting four times the amount for twice the money. Since the family is large, they will use that much soap powder.
2. The smaller milk is a better buy because most of the larger container will spoil before Juan can use it.
3. The single puppy is a better buy because the Bengles would probably not be able to take care of six puppies in an apartment.

Analyzing
Grog Is Rich! (page 89)
1. 16¢ 2. 26¢ 3. 20¢ 4. 30¢ 5. 92¢

Big Sale! (page 90)
Example 1:   **Example 2:**
the bear costs 5¢.   the ball costs 3¢.
the robot costs 7¢.   the game costs 10¢.

Unlock the Mystery (page 91)
Box #9

Pick a Winner (page 92)
Possible responses:
1. bird   6. ground
2. coat   7. ocean
3. plane   8. sun
4. ice   9. banana
5. worm   10. pillow

Clowning Around (page 93)
The pins are colored as follows:

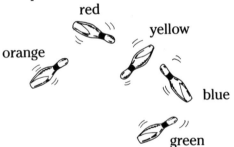

What's That Again? (page 94)
Possible responses:
1. trees 2. bone 3. spoon 4. snowman
5. sweater, coat 6. mice 7. broom
8. pools, lakes, ocean 9. teeth 10. pen, pencil, crayon

Same Things? (page 95)
1. not the same   7. not the same
2. not the same   8. same
3. not the same   9. not the same
4. not the same   10. not the same
5. same   11. same
6. not the same   12. same